The Knitted Curiosity Cabinet

Yvonne Marjot

Indigo Dreams Publishing

First Edition: The Knitted Curiosity Cabinet
First published in Great Britain in 2014 by:
Indigo Dreams Publishing
24, Forest Houses
Cookworthy Moor
Halwill
Beaworthy
Devon
EX21 5UU

www.indigodreams.co.uk

Yvonne Marjot has asserted her right under the Copyright, Designs and Patents Act 1988 to be identified as the author of this work.
©2014 Yvonne Marjot

ISBN 978-1-909357-34-1
British Library Cataloguing in Publication Data. A CIP record for this book can be obtained from the British Library.

This book is sold subject to the condition that it shall not, by way of trade or otherwise, be lent, re-sold, hired out, or otherwise circulated without the author's and publisher's prior consent in any form of binding or cover other than that in which it is published and without a similar condition including this condition being imposed on the subsequent purchaser.

Designed and typeset in Palatino Linotype by Indigo Dreams.

Cover design by Ronnie Goodyer at Indigo Dreams

Printed and bound in Great Britain by Imprint Academic, Exeter.
Papers used by Indigo Dreams are recyclable products made from wood grown in sustainable forests following the guidance of the Forest Stewardship Council.

Jeanette Marjot (née Bearman)
1938-2012

I couldn't have done it without you, Mum.

This volume would not have been possible without the support and encouragement of many wonderful people: Imran and the folk at Britwriters; Ronnie and Dawn at Indigo Dreams Publishing; An Tobar, the local arts centre in Tobermory, Isle of Mull, which is a wellspring of support for creative artists of all kinds; my readers and friends, for your vital constructive criticisms and affirmations; and my most constant supporters: my Dad, Mike, and my daughter, Elanor.

Previous works:

The Calgary Chessman Trilogy of novels,
Kindle Editions only at Amazon.co.uk
'The Calgary Chessman'
'The Book of Lismore'
'The Ashentilly Letters'

Herein find a collection of curios; an eclectic (meaning both selected and varied) mixture of topics: trees, lovers, moths, myth. It begins with the five poems that won the Adult Poetry Award at Britwriters Awards 2012. There's a selection of sonnets, a sprinkling of haiku, a homage to the beloved dead, a heady whiff of brine and seaweed and an intermittent, half-heard, track-skipping thread of humour, albeit often quite black. I hope you like it.

Yvonne Marjot 2013

CONTENTS

Sonnets for the Sea 11
I: Metaphorical Distance 11
II: Formalising the Atlantic 12
III: Like the Sea 13
Harbour 14
Clematis 14
How to Write Poetry (1) 15
Ash 16
For Neil 17
I dream of Jeannie 19
City of the Mind 21
Gorse Flowers 22
Ghost Story 23
How to Write Poetry (2) 25
Quarry 26
Ruins 27
Wings 28
Sunset 29
Fade to Grey 30
Benllech 31
Wales 33
How to Write Poetry (3) 34
Flower Child 35

Summer King	36
Vigil	37
Ordinary moments	39
Sitting at bus stops is free	40
It Rained All Night	41
The Lost Poetry Office	44
Thorn Apple	45
My Secret Life	47
Flyting by Text	48
Rapunzel	49
Ferry Haiku	51
Karikari fragment	52
Slightly Foxed	53
How To Write Poetry (4)	55
Three Mysteries	56
Ephemeral	57
Hallowed Halls	59
Crescendo	61
The Wind on the Hill	62
Carys and Dad in the Labyrinth	63
How to Write Poetry (5)	68

The Knitted Curiosity Cabinet

Sonnets for the Sea
Inspired by the exhibition of paintings by Bruce Killeen
(Sonnets of the Sea)

I: Metaphorical Distance

Out at farthest focus, drifting, peaceful:
Green ladled with mauve like a healing bruise.
Light lies heavy on the horizon; chooses
To lean its languid body westward. The pull
Of the rolling planet quickens, and the full,
Swelling, murmurous mass of the tide looses
The bonds of gravity, dropping the deep, pellucid,
Purpleness of light gracefully into the ocean's well.

Dipping my toe into the water, gasping
At the cold, desiring to go deeper and far,
I stare outward along the long divide
Of the horizon; the waves on the sand rasping
At the edge of the land, my feet, my heart:
Like this sea-coloured bruise I am trying to hide.

II: Formalising the Atlantic

Where will you go from here? You've measured exactly
The angle of sunlight that, striking the cloud layer,
Refracts through the prism of the horizon, neat and square,
A thousand shades of aquamarine; laying them delicately
End to end along the proper horizontal, modestly
Masked with shadow. With dividers and set square
You've drawn the perfect perpendicular, straight and set fair
To indicate the strict statistical limits of visual accuracy.

But how can you calculate clearly, precisely,
The creeping numbness of toes, cormorants, the stark
Face-slap of salt, the way the selkies sing?
Or the kick of the tiller against your wrist, turning nicely
Into the wind? Formal analysis misses the mark:
The poet is in this landscape. That changes everything.

III: Like the Sea

Why is a sonnet like the sea? For one,
When you start to search it recedes from you,
Seeping away towards the distant, blue
Hazy hover of light on the horizon.
Its going reveals deep clefts, exposed to the sun:
Vulnerable. Laid open to the view
Of the inner eye: arid fields of conflict; overdue
Reminders of other projects, left undone.

On a moment, while your back is turned: the change.
Moving effortlessly with the moon's quiet pull,
Thought washes back, inescapable.
The mind's tide rises. Words rearrange
Themselves. The ocean inspires: limpid, brimful
Of creativity. Not to write would be intolerable.

Harbour

Sunlight on the bay:
Golden promise of summer
Holds rain in its lap.

Clematis

Flower essences
Flow from the midnight pen of
My garden poet.

How to Write Poetry (1)

Make a list of rhyming words
And resonant phrases.
Add (sparingly) some alliteration;
Interesting assonances;
Sonorous synonyms;
 (but don't get carried away).

Carry it around in your pocket.
Refer to it at random moments.
Add instants of inspiration,
jotted notes, and favourite quotes.

If it goes through the wash by mistake,
Write another;
Or wash it on purpose to see
What fragments remain
To tempt your imagination.

After a month or two
Throw it away.
They are all clichés, anyway.

Ash
(with all respect to Richard Wilbur)

The High King of Summer, bent and ancient,
Stands by my back door, bearing his crown.
The lawn respects his shade and dies, turning brown
And dry. My sons turn cartwheels and fence
With plastic swords across the throne room, bent
On mayhem, hardly noticing the regal frame
That looms over the garden. When I named
The Old King I did not intend prescience.

As autumn comes I watch him overwhelmed;
A poor, creeping end for Odin's World Tree.
The King of Summer loses his crown and realm
To the usurping fungus: that sneaking, petty
Thief. Generous giver: as ash keys fall like confetti,
Will this year close the annals of the ash tree?

For Neil
(1930-2012)

Is it all over? Is that all there is?
The last Shuttle piggy-backed into a museum;
The planets sunk back into the star-flecked gloom,
And a cold look on the Moon's cold face?

In 1969 I was dragged out of bed
By my Dad, in the wee small hours,
To watch a bit of film on a tiny screen.
By the time I'd turned ten the last men
Had walked there. I have lived to see
The end of the Space Shuttle program, and the death
Of the first man to walk upon the Moon.

One October evening in 2012
I stood in my back garden, clutching a mug
Of coffee and jumping in place to keep warm:
Watching the round, yellow rise of the moon
That is now and always only the moon. My son
Asked me what on earth I was doing?
On earth. Grounded. Earthbound. Hugging the child
Who is a child of the world that does not go to the Moon.

'Saying goodbye,' I said: to the work, the plans
And the dreams. The last, reflexive kick
Of the Sixties; the anticlimactic end of an era;
The passing of a good man, and the close
Of the space program. I felt as though
Something in me was ending too. But then
I reminded myself of three far travellers.
Two are still travelling, voyaging into the dark,
Carrying what we thought was so important then:
The plan, the dream, our vision of what we are.

The third, this year, has made his final flight.
I raised my coffee cup to the moon and grinned
At its dear, familiar face. Of course the Moon
Is only the moon, and yet it seemed that if only
I reached out my hand I could take it to have and to hold.
I put the moon in my pocket and closed my eyes.
'Safe journey, Mr Armstrong.'

Neil Armstrong died on 25th August 2012. Not long afterwards, NASA confirmed that Voyager 1 space probe had left the heliopause. It is now crossing interstellar space.

I dream of Jeannie
(Jeanette Marjot, 1938-2012)

I dream of Jeannie,
Though your hair was not brown.
We had worn you down
With constant demands,
With fighting and whining;
Competing to be the favourite one.

Will you count five
Or six?
Or all the French exchange students
who passed through our home:
Do they count?

Your sisters and brothers,
Especially the young one,
So near our own age.
How many did you raise?

Then there are all the ones you taught,
In New Zealand;
In England.
How many remember the favourite teacher?
How many the scary disciplinarian?

We felt your disapproval,
As we ought;
But it was never as real as the stories,
The music, the plays:
All the things you taught us to do.

I dream of Jeannie,
Small in the big chair,
Holding on to life:
Living every moment, every day,
As you always have.
How can life let you go?
Your grip on it has been so strong:
You hold the planet together with your will,
As you held us together.
As you call us together now.
As you always will.

City of the Mind

One factor shared by fanatics of every creed,
The common thread that runs through all their plans,
Is hatred of knowledge: the evil, vital need
To control our minds, and thus our hearts and hands.

Hatred of knowledge sees icons of faith destroyed,
And children shot for wanting to go to school.
In place of it they offer us a void,
Empty of thought, slaved to another's will.

Greatest of all is hate of the written word;
The power to learn, to teach, to outgrow the past.
Knowledge is the weapon of tolerance, mightier than swords
Or bombs, but it is fragile and easily lost.

There is a city of the mind, a place where peace
Flourished, and commerce, and teachers were revered.
Thousands studied, regardless of creed or race,
And myriad strands of thought were debated and shared.

A city of trade and prosperity, greater than Troy,
Its wealth more precious by far than gems or gold:
Uncounted pieces of parchment, a scholar's joy;
A hundred thousand stories that wait to be told.

Have we the will to save this prize? I tell you,
This imaginary city is real: it is Timbuktu.

(In January 2013, rebel forces in Mali entered the city of Timbuktu and destroyed many of the buildings that had housed its famous libraries. The people of the city had worked for days beforehand, spiriting away as many documents as possible: some to the capital, Bamako, others into safe havens nearby. The world owes a debt of gratitude to those who saved this heritage.)

Gorse Flowers

"Bees do have a smell, you know, and if they don't they should, for their feet are dusted with spices from a million flowers."

from *Dandelion Wine*, by Ray Bradbury(1920-2012)

How strange it is that we recognise
That gorse flowers smell like coconut.
Bumblebees pollinate them, but
It seems altogether bizarre that, sated, they rise
Like drunk tourists from Caribbean bars,
Wending their erratic way from flower to flower,
Packing up brown paper bags for later,
And carrying with them the scent of Piña Coladas.

Was there once a time where some visiting explorer,
Red-faced and sunburnt, waded from the island surf,
And, mopping his face on the tattered rags of his shirt,
Eyeing the place in his first scientific foray,
Breathed the tropics' unmistakeable odour,
And said, 'how strange: coconuts smell like gorse flowers?'

Ghost Story

I walked with my brother on the downs,
Deep in the mist,
Early in the morning.

We had an old map, and a book of directions.
It gave the location of every stile
Along the way.

We were young (I was seventeen).
We didn't bother to take
A compass.

Also it was in the days
Before mobile phones.
(I said we were young!)

We did our best to follow the map.
The mist came down;
We got lost.

We put up our tent in an empty barn.
The next morning
It was full of cows.

We struck camp and set out again,
Looking for the way,
Hoping the mist would lift.

Cloud lay heavy on us and on the world.
We could hardly see each other.
Everything was lost.

We passed through a gap in the landscape:
A narrow slot
Between steep-sided hills.

We both stopped at the same moment.
Our conversation tailed off into silence.
We shivered.

Reaching out we gripped one another's hands.
With an effort of will
We forced ourselves forward.

Passing through the cleft the space opened out.
We walked on slowly.
The mist began to lift.

All the hairs on the back of my neck stood up.
We turned as one
To look behind us.

The mist streamed upward and the sun stabbed through.
We stood and stared
And laughed nervously.

Before us the hills we had struggled to pass:
Two great barrows,
In fog, on the downs.

How to Write Poetry (2)

A handful of words,
And seventeen syllables.
Now you're nearly there.

Quarry

Down in the quarry a wild light has been captured.
It slunk in on a dawn raid
Hunting rabbit, or perhaps fox,
But tumbled headlong into this pit.

Fragments of a million years grin from the quarry walls
As light tries its fingers on the crumbling handholds.

A murmur of wind stirs the air,
And light goes rocketing off across the landscape,
Careering into corners;
Trying to escape, but never quite making it.

Now it lies exhausted in the midday heat.

The sun blinks slowly in a staring sky.
Light spreads its tigerish length over everything,
Tongue lolling, patient.
Waiting.

Soon it will slink off,
One stripe at a time,
Switching its tail through the last western crevice.

Only its spoor will be left behind.

Ruins

We scrambled here last summer:
Clambered over tumbled stones at dawn, walked
On the wall of someone's house, sat and talked
As the sun came round and warmed us. Bees hummed
And the grass was alive with crickets. Overhead a raven
Kronked and wheeled, calling: 'strangers!' We thought
We'd healed the wounds, fought the last battle, bought
Time to rearrange the past: founded a haven
For two. Found hope. Do you remember?
It didn't last long. By September
You were back on the booze, on the way
To losing your job, giving it all away.
I never went back. Let the embers die
On the ruined hearth of any ordinary day.

Wings

Hebridean June:
Lepidopteran haiku
(read and be wary).

The fool on the hill
Is counting red wings carefully
(Burnet moth month).

June is my moth month.
Wherever thyme and heather bloom,
There my work is.

Left my new sandal
Sunk in oozing muck:
But I caught the butterfly!

Sunset

The sun sinks slowly in a pre-Raphaelite sky,
Painting in broad brushstrokes down the ecliptic:
All red-gold flame, flaunting its beauty,
Dragging its molten tresses behind it.

A cauldron of colours in tumbling fire;
Self-portrait in oils, skilfully blended,
Smearing itself boldly over the horizon:
Substance and spark expertly compounded.

After the fire, a wash of serenity.
Viridian indigo flows like a balm.
The golden head bows: a nod to eternity;
Night brings an endless moment of calm.

The canvas is shadowed now, all detail gone.
The artist will begin again tomorrow, at dawn.

Fade to Grey

The walls are grey, and the light
Barely touches her face.
For a moment she raises her eyes,
Then it all goes back to grey.

The window's a dismal blur;
There's hardly a sound in the place.
She's been sitting here unmoving,
Watching the memory play.

It's raining out there. The sound
Of the second hand marks out the day.
She must pull herself together.
She can't go on this way.

Other people endure this;
They seem to do it with grace.
Get up and walk out that door.
It's time to face the day.

She tells herself to move,
But her legs will not obey.
The hours wear on, and the light
Fades to a darker grey.

Outside is where it happened.
She can't go there again.
Inside it keeps on happening,
Over and over and over and over...

Benllech
Pant-y-Saer cromlech tomb, Anglesey

Stone cold,
Standing stark,
Sharp in frost-crack white:
The planet's frozen heart thrust up in
Speechless eloquence,
Stone silent.

Bitter air bites deep,
Behind a grey divide.
The winter sun promises nothing,
And delivers full measure.

Jutting into greyness,
The massive roof cradles a little space,
Once cloaked in earth,
Now open to sea-mist and stillness.

Here lay no Theban god-king
Given eternity by his known name,
Fresh on the lips of tour guides,
Or mangled by the tongues of tourists.

The unknown soldier and the
Pauper-dead of the workhouse
Had kindred here.
Here, nameless, lay small brown bones,
Cradled in earth and the memories of kin
Long since gone to earth themselves.

Take comfort –
We shall all come to that quiet place.

Slow wind bites ice-clad fingers,
And stops the breath in my mouth.
My hands have become stone,
But my heart is very warm.

Wales
(after Dylan Thomas)

Slate mountains glower,
Looming over the valley:
Thousand shades of grey.

Anglesey twilight:
White birds rocket skyward as
Mountains glow crimson.

How to Write Poetry (3)

Climb to the top of the garden at midnight;
Feet in wellies, cold, half-asleep.
The stars drift like plankton: miles deep
Shoals of tiny creatures; living light.

Trail your hand in the water, feel the chill
As phosphorescence coats your fingers. Lay
Your head back and let it swim, feel the sway
Of the endless ocean of night spilling over the hill.

Reach up your fist and drag the moon from the sky.
Smear it over the paper. Take a scrap
Of bitter dark, a sliver of frost, perhaps
A breath of emerald aurora, if you are lucky.

Pour the ink-black ocean over everything.
Paddle your fingers in luminescence, smear it
All over the page. Dry it in the slight,
Trembling, first clear breath of morning.

Bend down to wash in dew. Shake off the night.
Time to go in now: it's starting to get light.

Flower Child

One morning in spring the world gave me a gift:
A fairy child, changeling, bright and blithe.
Clear-eyed and fair, as golden as the flower
For which she was named, limb-light and lithe.

I woke to find her lying on my pillow,
A little cross-eyed; not looking: practising.
She startled, and her eyes fixed on my face.
I couldn't look away. My soul began to sing.

When I went to move my body reminded me:
Stiff-backed and sore, aching in every part,
I relived two days of hard work, pain and worry.
Worth every moment: true captor of my heart.

She walks in beauty, my daughter, evermore.
Golden flower of Lorien: Elanor.

Summer King

Ash,
Summer Tree:
Last of them all you stand bare,
Reaching over my garden.
Great, grey arms you hold out,
Claiming as much future territory as possible.

Huge, looming, swelling with life –
Holding it in check –
Summer dammed up in your purple buds:
Waiting.
Waiting for all the other trees to bloom and open.
Choosing your moment.

One morning, suddenly,
Greenness steals all the sunlight.
Shade claims my garden.
Grass yellows.
Biting visitors thrive in the cool dampness of your demesne.

High King of Summer:
You call it late, but there is no denying you.

A few weeks later you give it all back –
Generous, wasteful, profligate with your treasure.
I stand under a rain of heavy confetti:
Married to the king of summer,
Just as the year begins to turn.

Vigil

I was on the M74, heading South,
When dawn crept into the world,
Behind heavy cloud,
And a spattering of sleet.

On my way home:
Sorry Mum, running late again;
The story of my life.

Thumb tapping on the steering wheel
As I counted through the decades;
Invisible rosary beads slipping through my fingers.
Possibly not the most successful prayer –
I kept losing count and having to start again.

A sliver of sun shot into my eyes
And I thought – when it comes, this is the time
I would most like to die.
Just as the sun leaps into the sky,
And darkness gives way to the day.

I pulled in at Gretna for a break.
My chest felt tight
And I needed to stop and just breathe for a while.

It was there that Dad called me,
And told me you had died
A few moments before.

I sat down on the floor.
The invisible rosary beads
Scattered everywhere,
And my mind filled with questions
You will never be able to answer.

You were so strong.
You held on to life so tightly.
I didn't realise,
Until your hand slipped away from mine,
Just how hard I was holding on to you.

And I want to ask you:
 When the bridegroom came,
Were you ready?
Was your lamp filled with oil?
Did you see morning flame across heaven?
And were your eyes wide open?

Ordinary moments

On an ordinary day I sit at the window,
Looking out over the bay.
Boats rock gently against the tide,
Then settle as the wind dies.

The trees that frame the foreground
Are photographic stills,
Shot against a backdrop of distant haze.
Gulls slip across the view,
Gliding with effortless grace.

The clear-and-cloudy pattern of the sky
Lays down a wash of blue and grey,
And the long, slow afternoon light
Polishes the golden surface of the bay.

The water creeps and drizzles
Across the foreshore like treacle,
Its burnished surface seeping
In honey-thick ripples towards the sea wall.

Everything holds its breath.

An oystercatcher flashes past,
Its livery a black-and-white flame.
A whisper of wind silvers the water.
Time goes back to normal:
The same, never ordinary, day.

Sitting at bus stops is free
For my fellow poet, Lucienne Kim Flavell.

'If writers want inspiration,' Lucienne said,
'Try using public transport.' I'd like to,
But since I lost my job it's all I can do
To eat and keep a roof over my head.

Looking for work means daily, bitter frustration.
I save and stay fit by walking everywhere.
But the pleasure I miss the most, the worst loss to bear,
Is the simple, daily art of conversation.

I miss the workday round of chat and cheer,
And the bus driver's words and friendly morning smile.
If only I could find some company, just for a while.
Suddenly I have an amazing – a brilliant idea.

With a thermos of hot water I act on my realisation:
It's free to sit in the waiting room at the bus station.

It Rained All Night

It rained all night, drumming on the roof,
Seeping through my dreams and soaking the landscape.
The ditches are full of it, running down the road
And filling every hole. I try to escape
By going for a walk, ducking drips from the eaves,
Hat over my eyes and coat zipped tight.
The rain weights the leaves: the same load
Burdens my soul as I walk, eyes open to the grey light.

I have cried a million tears, and this month
It seems the earth has cried the same.
Day by dark day the sodden sky
Has never dried, although I know the sun came
And walked in fields of blue and cloud
Once, while proud snow-bonneted
Mountains emerged like white teeth,
Studding the wide open mouth of the horizon.

A winter of leaves, as I trudge up the lane,
Line the new drain running deep and clean.
I watch for cars: the bane of walkers;
One comes, and I'm caught – pause and lean
To straddle the ditch, give it room to go by.
At the hilltop lay-by I turn into the track
That leads on to the forest and run.
Once I reach the summit I'll turn and go back.

At the quarry on the hill I pause and look,
Remembering walks here long ago;
Two small boys, in jackets and boots
Leaping and whooping, braving the snow
New-melted to jump in every pool;
The cruelty of brothers: play as war;
The elder winning (as always) until
The little one stooped, stumbled, jumped too far

And vanished! The surface closed over his head.
The water bled darkness like ink, shuddered,
And was still. For a long moment
I stood frozen, then shed gloves and leapt forward.
Plunging both arms through the skin of the world,
I groped in the cold, frantic, afraid:
My fingers found fabric; I gripped his hood
And pulled, wrenching him back into the day.

Helpless I crouched, knees grinding the gravel:
Pulse unravelling, heart in my throat.
Hardly able to breathe as I cried,
Wild-eyed I caught him up in my coat.
His brother came running and I clasped him close,
Held them both, continually
Reliving the loss, slow to realise
The crisis was done, as they tried to comfort me.

All the way down the hill they cheered
And chattered, fearless, telling the story:
Turning the endless moment of fear
Into a hilarious family comedy.
But I've never forgotten the moment he fell;
Pitched into the well so darkness took him,
And I hurled myself forward, into the black,
To claim him back from the grip of the other side.

The veil between worlds is gossamer thin;
A silken skin over the black unknown:
No way back who enter in.
Now again I have been shown it.
We spent long enough on the waiting game,
Watching the flame dwindle and sink.
So many times I saw rally and recovery,
Lovely to claim every moment snatched from the brink.

I spent those years learning how to grieve,
How to leave, how you would leave me.
We talked out all the 'shoulds' and 'oughts'.
I thought the tie would gently slip free.
I was ready; thought myself prepared
As you fared over the edge of the wild.
But again and again I find myself stood at that bourn,
Trying to learn to live as a motherless child.

The Lost Poetry Office

A thin layer of sand coats the floor.
It's worth checking.
Every grain is a word left out,
A preposition that disturbed the rhythm,
Or a misplaced rhyme.

Behind the door
A selkie sits, sulking.
If she could find her skin
She would go back to the sea,
But she doesn't know it is filed under 'P'.

This cabinet washed ashore,
Coated in limpets, battered
By storms: I have a feeling
Each shell hides a thing
That may still be living.

That day you couldn't find paper or
A pen in your pocket:
Had the words in your head,
But on the bus they slipped away.
They're here somewhere.

I'm sorry,
I would look, but
I can't help you.
If it's found poems you're looking for,
You'd better try next door.

Thorn Apple

Moonflowers; Angels' Trumpets; Jimsonweed;
Thorn Apple; Devil's Trumpet; Witches' Weeds;
Datura.

Plant them in the sun; keep the soil dry:
If they like your garden they will self-seed
Everywhere.

Tell your children not to touch them.
Tell your children. They are beautiful.
Dangerous.

Atropine makes witches fly, shamans dance.
They are oh-so-beautiful. Toxic.
Hallucinogenic.

Giant leopard moth caterpillars
Eat the leaves safely, eagerly:
Adapted.

They do not, apparently, have trouble
Distinguishing reality from hallucination.
Amnesia

Is not a symptom observable in the species.
Although, from our perspective, who can say
Surely,

That caterpillars do not hallucinate
When stuffed to the gills with neurotoxic
Atropine?

They sleep off *Datura* narcosis,
Spending a few weeks out of circulation:
Chrysalis.

Then, like witches in fake-fur coats,
Arise and mount their hallucinatory broomsticks,
Spiralling

Out of the ordinary, *Datura* rising
Over the ripening seed cases:
Thorn Apple.

My Secret Life

In my secret life I hold a key
That hides in the pocket of every coat I wear.
No-one can possibly know that it is there,
But my searching fingers find it and draw it to me.

It opens a door made of metal, or plywood, or stone
Carved by craftsmen, or water; or woven by witches,
Hidden behind a tapestry of invisible stitches.
I can step through only when I am alone.

There is a room made wholly of mother-of-pearl;
A garden inside a water-drop; a spiral
Staircase; a purple dome with astronomical
Ceiling; savannah; a library; a castle.

I never know what I will see until I look.
In every room there is a pencil and a book.

Flyting by Text

Come on.
Put 'em up.
You know you want to.

I'll show you mine if
You'll show me yours.

Something nice now.
Greeting card pretty.
I dare you.

Now take some time:
Show me a rhyme

Call that a poem?
What happened to
The metre
Halfway through?

Oh...
Flirting.
You meant flirting?
Darned auto-correct!

Rapunzel

Today I bought
The last chocolate croissant.

The man in line behind me
Had been waiting
To buy it for his girlfriend.
She was pregnant.
Nothing else would do.

I remember what that was like:
Rapunzel's mother craving nothing
But the perfect lettuces
In the witch's garden
(Her own slug-eaten versions
Just not the same).

Did Rapunzel in her tower
Know, as she kicked against
The restraining wall of the womb,
That in eighteen years she would be
Doing it again:
Struggling to leave the narrow world of childhood
And find her woman's self?

Never mind the version
Where the mother is also the witch,
(The life-giver transmuted into
The wicked, controlling obsessive
Who cannot let her little girl grow up)
And the whole story folds in upon itself
In the way that real life does.
In her turn, Rapunzel will crave lettuces.

Haven't we all done it?
Sent our man out,
Regardless of consequences,
To find the One thing:
Whatever it is that is needed?

Strawberries in winter.
The wolf skin cloak.
A kept promise.
Proof of true love.
A perfect lettuce.

The last chocolate croissant.

Ferry Haiku

My prosaic morning
To the supermarket
Past Lismore lighthouse.

Oban afternoon:
Sapphirine sun-flecked water;
Three ferries dancing.

Up the Sound of Mull:
Moon jellies churned in the wake;
Seven porpoises.

In the rising tide:
Cormorants with feet awash,
Dancing on the spot.

Balanced impossibly
On the substanceless sea:
Hidden rock with seal.

Karikari fragment

I dreamed myself walking on a desert island:
White sand, white sky,
Sea impossibly blue.

Treading the bones of time, ground down,
A scallop-shell cupped my heel;
Blood sprang from splintered edge driven deep.

I dreamed myself awake and you beside me,
Drowning deep in
Light impossibly clear.

We turned like dolphins in the cool, green sea of morning,
Entering the island-ocean of the heart's delight.

I woke to bitter greyness:
Eyes wet but mouth dry.

Slightly Foxed

In the 60s, new minted, it was all about play.
I had no time for the shock of the new:
I ran everywhere, when I wasn't dancing.
I loved to sing;
And to read, and read, and read.

Chapter two: a sea change.
Over sea: six weeks of the world's oceans
Brought me a blue and green world.
There is nowhere more beautiful than Aotearoa.
Tino nui te aroha.

The 70s, too, were for reading. Everywhere.
There was nothing I did not want to know.
In time, I thought I would understand it all.
At the same time, we played at survival:
Planning, always, for the day the Bomb would fall.
Some of us hoarded iodine and medical texts,
Or constantly practised essential skills.
We were all going to be doctors, farmers or scientists:
There would be no place for artists or musicians
In the post-nuclear scramble.

I thought of that often while I sat in my room,
Strumming a borrowed guitar,
And composing miserable songs in a minor key:
Endless, hopeless love songs to the boy
Who was such a good friend.
Adolescence was gloriously bittersweet.

The 80s arrived in a rush of independence,
Lurching compulsively from one experience to the next.
Life leapt into my lap and consumed me.

I found myself captivated by
The most beautiful human being on the planet:
Astonished that she should have chosen me
To be her mother.
I found and lost my best and greatest friend:
Our connection a casualty of fear.
Never forget (never, *never* forget) to tell him that you love him,
Over and over again, as many times as it takes.
Too many times is not enough.

The last years of the century were the strangest:
Struggling with loneliness;
Writing my way from chapter to chapter,
Knowing that no-one would read the whole tale.
Two boys in as many years,
And the beginning of a decade of loss and decay:
Struggling from day to day, as slowly
The bindings began to disintegrate and the story
Started to fall apart.

Suddenly, a new start, a new postcode,
And the lottery fell in my favour:
Beginning the slow process of putting the pieces back together,
One suture at a time.
(Plumped out and perked up,
Like a ragdoll with new stuffing,
Until the whole mixed metaphor was shoved back
onto the shelf.)

Carefully, painstakingly sewn back together:
A tribute to the bookbinder's art.
Still in the old dust-covers.
Slightly foxed,
And going for a song.

How To Write Poetry (4)

You really need to have some rhymes
For limericks and valentines.
For other kinds of verse and stuff,
Not so much.

Three Mysteries

In these hands, these very ordinary hands,
I have held three mysteries of Earth.
Held, without touching, the mystery of birth
Three times: the magic number. In other lands,
I have clasped, without clutching, a stranger's
Hand and called him lover, husband: the lost half
Of my sundered whole. And let go; sent forth;
Set free the link: soul singing its full range.

These high changes, these low, my heart has rung.
Only once have my hands held a trembling soul
In the moment it slipped its bonds, as I clung
A moment to the bedside, humbled by a soul leaping wholly
Free, ringing in the changes, speaking in tongues untold
As, before me, the mystery of the world unfolded.

Ephemeral

The tide is coming in.
It is coming in.

My son has made a boat out of sand.
All the shape of it,
Curving prow,
Broad stern,
Thwarts and gunwales:
All made of sand.

He is the captain of the moment.
His boat breasts the waves,
Heading towards the sunset.

The sea pushes back.
The bow is smooth now
And thinning.
He pulls sand out from the centre
And piles it onto the front and sides.
Too little.
Too late.
Too bad.

Falling back, he begins again.
A round castle;
A hastily constructed wall.
The lord of the manor takes his place
As the slow spin of the planet
Turns the castle
Into the path of the ocean.

Frantically he keeps building,
Digging deeper,
Piling higher,
As the waves slop over his perimeter.

He crouches over the curtain wall,
Protecting it with his body,
Holding his hands up to stop
The inexorable advance of his foe.

I dance in the waves,
Hopping from foot to foot,
Soaked to the knee, then the thigh,
Snapping shot after shot
With my cheap camera:
Trying not to let my shadow,
Shaking with laughter,
Spoil the picture.

Later we upload the result.
153 frames.
In a fast slide show
They are almost as good as a film,
And much funnier.

Again and again we watch the boat overwhelmed,
The castle breached:
Canute on his throne
Defying the big sea.

And on the little screen of the PC,
Right here,
Right now,
The tide is coming in.

Hallowed Halls
(Blaenafon coal mine, Wales)

The hollow hills were made by men,
Delving deep into the bitter dark.
Long they wrought in silence
The miners' mystery:
Carving the wealth of Faerie to feed
The insatiable beast of industrialisation.
Kingdoms of black-lung and silicosis
Gnawed out of the roots of mountains;
Tossing lost lives aside
Into the dark god's gaping maw.

Into the hollow hills we come,
Marvelling at the silence:
An echoing quiet deep in the
Thick, enveloping dark.
When the eyes adjust,
Shyly,
Out of the corners,
Dim shapes hesitate at the edge of sight.

Dispossessed denizens of Faerie?
Or the bemused ghosts of
Young mothers' sons,
Left behind pitfalls or pinned
Under fallen timbers,
Remembering the daylight only when
A tourist's torch
Catches the kicked up dust?

The miners' mystery enters my lungs until I
Cough my guts out,
Thinking I empathise.
But the sharp, clean air of the mountains
Awaits me,
And I need not stay in the dark.

This goblin kingdom is peopled
By restless ghosts;
And those who once mourned them
Lie under dark themselves,
Buried in the earth of Australia or Patagonia:
Inhabiting the hollow hills of another country.

Crescendo
(2013 was the centenary of Stravinsky's Rite of Spring)

Cognitive dissonance;
Sonorous pulse.
The driving rhythm of strings
Resonates in my blood;
And the evocative
Nearly-melody
In the woodwinds
Finds a sympathetic harmonic
In the net of nerves pricking,
Snapping,
Scintillating
In my fingertips.

This year the winter
Seemed endless:
Day after day of dry cold,
Cracking lips and striking
Frozen fingers with chilblains.
On a day in April,
Much like any other,
The wind changed.
A wild air played above my head,
Uttering a plangent melody
In dissonant harmonics.
The whole percussion section
Banged on my ears,
And ushered in the spring.

It was worth waiting for.

The Wind on the Hill

Carry me down and lay me
Where you will.
My heart will lie quiet,
Wherever you put me,
And I'll not stir.

I will turn away,
Into stillness of air:
Drowsy days;
An endless season of peace.

There'll be no more tears.
The words and the fire
Will go to earth
And rest serene.

In dappled days and dark,
In the corner of the picture,
At the limit of your vision:
You'll not find me where you look.

But I will still be here,
In the wind on the hill.

Carys and Dad in the Labyrinth

When his soldiers had finished with you,
they dumped you down into the pit with me.
I was filled with joy to find you still breathing.

Later, when I began to understand,
I wanted to kill you myself.
Or to kill myself.
 I had not the strength for either,
but you were astonishingly strong.

Slowly you began to live.
Your tenacity binds me here:
in no way can I bring myself to leave you.

While I had thought myself eternally alone I had begun to work.
Plans were well underway.
 I had almost all the materials I needed,
and my escape had become a viable possibility.
Now I have to consider
whether the plan can be made to work for two.

More time is needed.
Time I don't have.
If only I had been ready earlier.
But there is no point in dwelling on might-have-beens.

Each day you drag your body a little further in the dust.
There is still some blood, but not so much.
The pain of your twisted torso enters my eyes
and wrenches my heart.

I know you do not feel it.
Your determination to move yourself fills me with pride,
but I turn away:
to watch you is unbearable.

How women love to talk: I've never understood it.
I remember nights by your cradle,
escaping your mother's constant chatter
by hiding in the quiet nursery to watch you sleep;
Her soft voice, just audible, like a little bird,
her friends like a bright-plumaged flock, twittering.

How I had prayed for a son: someone to follow me in my work,
to achieve with me,
to stand on my shoulders and reach for the sun.
How I longed for an equal, to share the work.
And all the time, I planned for you a gentle path,
a safe life:
warmth and comfort and ordinariness.

I kept you safe and homely:
your mother taught you the women's arts,
cuddled and caressed you,
fussed over you,
sent you to me from time to time
to show me your accomplishments:
a song, a handful of cakes, a piece of needlework.

I was proud of you.
I was, my dear,
but I did not allow you into my laboratory.
Daddy's boring old work: not for you.
When death took mother and son from me
you became my strength and support.
The work went on while you kept our home.

You were dutiful and obedient,
and I loved you for it,
even as I grieved over and over
for the wife lost and the son not born.

When they came for me with shouts of 'traitor' and 'terrorist';
when they dragged me before the court
and read out my journals,
put lies in my mouth,
tortured 'the truth' from me
and banished me here to the depths of this broken darkness,
I held to the candle-flame of your image.
I loved to think of you,
docile and womanly,
keeping the house against my return.

I didn't know.
By all the Gods, daughter, I didn't know.

Over the weeks your face has lost its swollen look,
and I have become accustomed to its permanent distortions.
My girl still looks out from above the broken cheek-bones,
but your eyes are full of questions.

You ask about my work, my feelings, the past.
You want to find yourself again by refitting all the broken pieces.
But too many are missing.

I cannot bear all the talk.
All the dragging about;
the calluses on your forearms and elbows;
the pathetic attempts to make a home amid the rubble:
or the clarity of your gaze as you turn your face to me,
illuminated in a stream of dusty sunlight fallen from the heights.

I take refuge in my work as (I admit it) I always have.
It has taken months to gather all these feathers,
to distil the adhesive,
to lay them out so carefully by length
and to devise the attachments.
I must guess your mass and the effect
of the dead weight you drag behind you.

We will make only one attempt.
You will never walk again,
but I swear I can make you fly.

When all is ready I try to explain to you:
the mechanisms, the physics of it,
the risks and constraints of the method;
but you don't seem to take it in.
Perhaps you are sulking
because I wouldn't talk to you about feelings,
or the past,
or reasons.
We haven't time for that!

A son would have listened.
A son would have implicitly understood the mechanics:
The need to maintain a constant altitude once airborne;
The risks of salt water,
or the heat of the sun.

A son would have been beside me,
learning from the beginning,
not kept to the kitchen arts
and protected from knowledge and risk.

When I held you back I thought I was keeping you safe.
I only wanted what was best for you.

Now, as we drag ourselves slowly upward,
clinging to this rock chimney,
inching towards the gleam of sunlight from far overhead,
I begin to wonder.

When we emerge into the light and spread our wings,
will you keep to the middle path?
Will you follow me in duty and humility,
obeying my instructions so carefully designed to keep you safe,
using my gift to raise your broken body
to the tasks of normal life?

Or have you been listening after all?
Have you truly understood the miracle of flight?

Will I watch you strive for the sun at last,
casting off the chains of earth:
twisting in burning grace
as you break all your bonds at once and fall,
fall into myth?

My daughter, I do not understand you.
I begin to know that I never shall.

How to Write Poetry (5)

Go on. Just do it.
You know you really want to.
Best wishes, Yvonne.

Indigo Dreams Publishing Ltd
24, Forest Houses
Cookworthy Moor
Halwill
Beaworthy
Devon
EX21 5UU